PIONEERING

Also by Susan Eisenberg

It's a Good Thing I'm Not Macho
We'll Call You If We Need You:
Experiences of Women Working Construction

PIONEERING

Poems from the Construction Site

SUSAN EISENBERG

ILR Press, an imprint of Cornell University Press
Ithaca and London

First published 1998 by Cornell University Press.

Printed in the United States of America.

Library of Congress Cataloging-in-Publication Data

Eisenberg, Susan.
Pioneering : poems from the construction site / Susan Eisenberg.
        p.   cm.
    ISBN 0-8014-8526-6 (paper : alk. paper)
    1. Women construction workers—Poetry. 2. Construction
industry—Poetry. I. Title.
PS3555.I8438P56   1998
811' .54—dc21   97-43452

Cornell University Press strives to utilize environmentally responsible suppliers and materials to the fullest extent possible in the publishing of its books. Such materials include vegetable-based, low-VOC inks and acid-free papers that are also either recycled, totally chlorine-free, or partly composed of nonwood fibers.

Paperback printing
10 9 8 7 6 5 4 3 2 1

for my father

who shared with me
his passion
for the grace of language

Contents

from *It's a Good Thing I'm Not Macho* (1984)

Acknowledgments

SOME OF THE POEMS in this volume, or earlier versions of them, first appeared in the following books and magazines:

1 in 3: Women with Cancer Confront an Epidemic. Ed. Judy Brady. Pittsburgh: Cleis Press, 1991. "The Appointed Day," "Nuclear Medicine Clinic."
Canadian Dimension: "The Crew," "Partner #2," "Partner #9."
Equal Means: "Did She Tell You About Running Pipe?"
Hanging Loose: "Hanging In, Solo."
Harbor Review: "Companion," "Through the Ceiling, Maiden Voyage."
Prairie Schooner: "Partner #3," "The Summer She Decided to Quit," "UnWelcome Mats at the Construction Site."
Radical America: "Partner #1," "Partner #7," "Pioneering."
Seattle Review: "Tell Me."
Sing Heavenly Muse!: "Partner #5," "Partner #6," "Work Fantasy."
Slipstream: "Force Equals Distance Times Weight."
Tradeswomen: "Exposure," "Following the Blueprints."

It's a Good Thing I'm Not Macho was originally published in 1984 by Whetstone Press (245 Pelham Road, Amherst, Mass. 01002) in a letterpress edition of 1000.

Deepest thanks to Denise Levertov, Tom McGrath, Tom Wayman, Sandra Shreve, Susan Doro, Larry Levis, Alan Williamson, Thomas Lux, and the MFA Program for Writers at Warren Wilson College community —all of whom have nurtured and nudged this writing; and especially to Eleanor Wilner, who read through and commented on the entire manuscript. And to the many tradeswomen who have been both muse and grounding rod.

Introduction

FOR ALMOST TWO DECADES I have been writing poems drawn from the same material, women in the construction industry. The earliest poems, those that became the chapbook *It's a Good Thing I'm Not Macho,* published in 1984 by Whetstone Press, were originally private responses to the experiences of my apprenticeship years, 1978-1982, when I was learning my trade as an electrician.

After federal affirmative action guidelines opened construction gates to women in 1978, I was among six women who entered the four-year apprenticeship training program of Boston's Local 103 of the International Brotherhood of Electrical Workers (IBEW). Under a great deal of scrutiny, the five of us who remained at the end of our first year recognized that our survival was intertwined and—though isolated on different jobsites—we coaxed, advised, supported and sometimes bullied each other to ensure that we graduated together as the first women in our local to achieve journeylevel status. Like many other women breaking barriers then in historically male occupations, we believed that the path we were opening would not only widen but eventually become an ordinary road. In construction, that did not happen; women's numbers have yet to go beyond 2 percent of the workforce.

It was only when *It's a Good Thing I'm Not Macho* was published and I began to receive letters from our counterparts learning other trades or living in other regions of the country that I realized how strong the commonality of experience among us was. The ongoing dialogue I have had with the national community of tradeswomen over the years has been invaluable to me as a writer. It was in response to comments of an ex-firefighter after a reading I gave in Berkeley in the mid-eighties—when the toll of never-breaking-beyond-the-pioneering-phase was becoming evident—that I realized how understated I had been in my poems about the difficulties and hostility we faced. I went home and wrote the poem "Pioneering."

My writing changed, as it did again when I began to interview women carpenters, electricians, ironworkers, painters and plumbers for what would become the nonfiction book *We'll Call You If We Need You: Experiences of Women Working Construction.* The poems of *Shifting Earth* that open this volume reflect the more longterm concerns of practicing a skilled trade at journeylevel in an industry that is inherently dangerous— without any longer assuming that a commitment to women's full participation in the industry is forthcoming from either government, unions, or contractors.

These poems have had their own journeys. In 1986, I was invited to participate in the Split Shift Colloquium on New Work Writing in Vancouver, British Columbia, sponsored by the Vancouver Industrial Writers Union. Each night poets read about their jobs in factories, classrooms, railroads, offices, logging camps and computer rooms. There I met other writers who shared my belief that what we do for daily work shapes— sometimes strengthening, sometimes crippling—our physical bodies, our emotions, our aspirations.

Many of these poems have appeared in *Tradeswomen* magazine which has always recognized the important role of culture in breaking any boundaries, publishing the poetry and fiction of tradeswomen in almost every issue. Some of these poems are part of *NOT on a SILVER PLATTER,* an interactive installation of stories, poems, soft sculpture and found objects that spent a summer at the AFL–CIO George Meany Center for Labor Studies in Silver Spring, Maryland. I am pleased to have these poems come together in this collection and thank my editor, Fran Benson, for creating this opportunity.

Shifting Earth

Following the Blueprints

To the open possibility
of steel against sky
we weld, bolt and strap

wide staircases of marble, arched
skylights, commanding views

serviced by windowless corridors
where ceilings hang low, as though
the ones who will push carts and carry trays
are unusually small or
prefer to scurry, like mice
in closed dark spaces

or as though
extra headroom might give them
                              ideas.

Pioneering
for the tradeswomen of '78

She had walked into their party uninvited
wedging a welcome mat in the doorway
for other women she hoped would
follow along soon.
            The loud ones argued
to throw her out immediately. Even her supporters
found her audacity annoying. But once they saw
she mingled with everyone
drank American beer
kept conversations going during awkward silences

and was backed up by law
the controversy
           calmed.

She surprised them.
She was reliable. She always gave her best.
She was invited back.
She became a regular—
        always on the fringe
        expected to help out
               just a little more.

When she stopped coming
they were confused. Why now? Hadn't she
challenged custom? stared down rumors? ingratiated herself
years ago? so that now her presence was only
mildly discomforting. She never explained.

4

After all those years hurling back cannonballs
womanizing the barricades firing
only if she saw the whites of their eyes
it was the lonesomeness
                              of pioneering
that broke her resistance.

All those silences
            about what mattered
            most in her life
had worn her

like the slow eating away of acid on metal:
the damage only visible over time.

Transients

Walking onto jobsites lugging
toolbox   gear   and a lunch
to be eaten at morning coffee

we make home   by conversation
gathered around some appliance
hauled back from the dumpster;

settling in—even on a long job—with only
our place on a bench and a nail hook
we've driven in ourselves.

Gaping earth   to steel   to trim—
the decks of players
get shuffled and reshuffled.

Hard times: almost
anything
traded to avoid layoff.

Did She Tell You About Running Pipe?

Racks of them   slicing the vault air
spinning   leaping   kicking
their powerfully rounded thighs in perfect
unison   like an ensemble of Russian dancers
soaring robustly across a long stage.
Muscular limbs synchronized
        dive into switchgear
        thrust up through concrete!

Woman   whose hands for millenniums
        shaped dough into bread
        shaped clay into pots
        shaped plant fiber into cloth
apprenticed to Vulcan Himself
practiced all His secrets—
now   she runs pipe
and lights the Heavens with laughter.

Hazard: Writing at Work

The corner of cardboard
torn from a carton
and safely tucked
in a back pocket
with your scribbled line

I regret to say
has been rinsed washed
spun and tumbled and
though warm and fluffed
is quite   blank.

I have left it
folded with the laundry.
Perhaps its shape
will remind you
of your words.

Force Equals Distance Times Weight
for the pipefitter apprentice at the Hynes

Consider this skin-encased bundle of fat and muscle
each intricate organ protected by bones
known to splinter on impact: a man.

Consider the marble stairs patiently
waiting   smooth   hard   cold   below.

Consider the distance: fifty-five feet
not the carefully-arranged
landing of a diver or parachutist

a come-as-you-are unexpected arrival
human body meeting metamorphic rock.

Once it begins this
unruly fall from the steps of a ladder
past where a guardrail will be installed
within the hour

                    the details
of his particular life   step back
      the wife   the new baby
      each kindness each wildness—
      everything that will be chewed over
      later so many times—
until this delicate collision of physics
                              and fate

lands.

Jurisdiction
(at the Convention Center Job)

A few feet from the conference hall filled
with Dentists (a Grand Opening
PR scheme to camouflage construction—
the job well past deadline) a fitter
fell 3 stories onto stone

and lay there
30 minutes

while first the ambulance circled 'round
and 'round unmarked doors, then medics
threaded the stretcher through a maze
(not to disrupt the con convention).

Jokes turned mutinous.

So the foreman read a memo from the boss
ordering electricians—if one of *us* should tumble—
to drop our tools, rush outside, wave
the ambulance down and escort EMTs
to the fallen crewmate. Unstated

but understood: work stoppage for the neardeath
of any other trade—plumber, painter, mason or
that fitter again—would not be authorized.

From Up North Architect William Strickland Designs the New Orleans Mint, 1832

After the Capitol, Naval Home
and a Mint in Philadelphia   another Mint

was a zipzap draw-it-in-your-sleep-
and-sign-your-name-er. New Orleans

fortunate   to be favored
with a Strickland plan   perfect

for the rocksoil of Philly where
it would have stood up straight.

For more than a century and a half
Delta tradesmen   had work.

Partner #1

It was him and men like him
refashioned that skyline. A remnant
from more colorful days when
everyone answered to a name like
the Buzzard or Brownwater or Stinky
or Doctor Doom. Days more difficult
than these, when the work was done
all by hand and it was not so easy
a girl could do it. More
dangerous days when you saw
men flattened like pancakes fried like chickens
sailing like kites to their death
and no one came out to check on why.

Reduced now to the easier tasks
saved for old-timers and the partners
no one else will accept   his eyesight
no match for tiny print on a motor nameplate
he growls and hisses and shoves a lifetime
of lessons on any student willing:

gold   fool's gold   pebbles
bundled together in one sack.

Partner #2

From the paper mill she remembered him
in gauzy pastels blue   pink   green
like the foam overflowing calf-deep as he
taught her to wire motors   hang cable tray—

until the Christmas party confession of his
obsession with her breasts as she labored
beneath him. No longer remembered   only in pastels.

Partner #3

She smelled dynamite on his shirt;
men on the crew noticed
nothing peculiar.
She moved cautiously, lit
no matches. When she turned him down
for an after-work drink she heard the fuse

ignite. He stopped
calling her by name, just *Waitress!*
and gave his coffee order in strict
detail   *Bagel toasted   Not grilled*
            Orange juice   With ice
Whenever an elevator door closed leaving them
alone for a caged ride he recounted
hunting stories: deer drenched in blood. Still
like his too-conscious politeness or his
eerily frozen smile these were hardly
sufficient evidence—he a journeyman, she
an apprentice—for complaining out of place.

The afternoon he threatened death
by strangulation
         for the nurse
         and the medical director's wife
reciting their crimes (so like her own) as he
stared into her face, the whole while throwing
retrieving, throwing, retrieving, throwing

an open knifeblade against a wooden ladder,
staring, staring into her face
as he threw the open knife that day

she risked   requesting a transfer.

Partner #4

He: a just–get–started zealot.
She: a plan–the–job–out dogmatist.

They locked horns and bickered
right up to the annulment.

Partner #5

By reputation: Shop Gentleman, the one who won't
embarrass the owner if courteous conversation
is required. She expects an easy day.

A vault full of eight-foot fluorescents to hang
they stand in separate lifts, movements
synchronized, hoist each fixture
     drill and bolt overhead,
     twist splices, cover, lamps,
down for the next and up again—how much
easier it might be if he   spoke to her.

As she squeezes fingers
through a tiny opening to grab wires
she teases about the convenience
of small hands.

I can do anything in this business he snarls
and again: silence.

Partner #6

Foreman diplomacy paired them up
first 5 minutes on the job

avoiding any refusals to partner with
the 1 female   the 1 black. They shrugged:

the rejection   their respite from
feigning deafness   and deference.

Brought their homeselves in. Got themselves
comfortable, work and talk flowing like

wire through well-laid pipe, or the tunes
they sometimes sang. One by one

the crew found cause to buzz closeby
like homesick travelers drawn to warmth.

Partner #7

To him, she was a novelty:
a Lady Mechanic
with more years in the business
than him. Their partnership: a gauntlet
flung before his manhood
to bugle calls of testosterone.

To her, he was like
hundreds she had met already
their partnership just another
tedious test of patience. Boredom
hung over her head like a black hood
until she began to look forward

to her bathroom breaks that became longer
and more frequent each day.
The Ladies Room her private tower:
a sanctuary from those jokes—
so clever to him—and not one
new to her.

Partner #8

Her reputation preceded her—how she
always carried her lawyer's number
in her pocket and—you give
her any trouble—*smack*
she'll have you in court.
He was trembling when they met

which threw her off-track.
Not 'til the afternoon she was out
and coffee break became Jew Joke Cabaret
did she catch his ID. He bought
a Star of David necklace
on his way home; wore it next day
so everyone could see. Unafraid
to cross swords with the Legion of Sheep
he was the Brave Knight she'd
years ago given up expecting.

Partner #9

Checked each other out over lunch
trading barbs about b.a.'s and bosses,
returning late just to make their
I don't give a shit positions
clear.

Checked each other out again over work
matching each other stride for stride
dirt for dirt grunt for grunt
decision for decision
just to show they had a certain
pride even if they didn't
give a shit.

As the months relaxed, they stopped
suiting up in ornery postures—
left them in the gangbox with the raingear
and began to uncover their crisscross
of roots in a decade long past
     when he refused to load a ship
     and she left her marked path
seeding a friendship that defied harsh soil.

The Crew

She sketched each one onto paper,
shuffled them like playing cards, then
lay them face up for a Tarot reading
or stood them in a row like the Red Queen's army
or fanned them in her hand. Whatever way

they never came out right. Shuffle again
lay them out. Shuffle again into a fan.
No matter how she rearranged
or shuffled she never wanted
to put her own face card among them
but held it nestled close against her.

For Money, at the Hotel

someone every morning pulled out the chair for Mr. K
so he could eat his bowl of berries and bran flakes;

someone polished fingerprints
from brass banisters;

someone removed brown leaves
from lobby bouquets;

a carpenter made a straight wall curved
to match an armoire's turn;

me and John, we crawled a wire
through forty yards of spidernests
to re-switch the canopy lights

and from 10-foot ladders watched a black Buick
aim high-speed for the doorman
who stood still for the regular's tip.

The Walk Home

Once, her day's breakpoint:
that stroll from trainstop home,
the workday's tight grip on the senses
shaken loose by the time she turned the last
corner, said *hello* to Mr. Bartley working,
as always, in his garden, asked
after his peonies and his rheumatism.

Now more a canter than walk
barely a breath between trolley door
snapping behind and front door
swallowing her into dinner bath and story:
 What'd you do in school today?
 Don't eat the peas frozen!
 C'mon kids! Set the table, one of you!
Even asleep children breed work: lunches to be made,
laundry washed and put away. Not realizing until
finally under the covers herself:

Mr. Bartley not in his garden
a week now. Ring his bell
 tomorrow.

Exposure

1) A Word

Malignancy. Before the *m*
touches my lips the syllables
multiply in my mouth
and metastasize across my face.

At just   the chance
I turn mute.

2) Nuclear Medicine Clinic

No cheerful team of nurses welcomes
us, only a receptionist who asks about
insurance, then directs us to hard plastic seats
where we wait to be called by name.
All the comfortable chairs, bouquets,
coffee tables with magazines are up in Maternity
where curtains open out to sky.

Here in the basement bunker medications
are stored behind lead shields
and those who touch us
wear special rings and badges.
We glance at each other and guess
our rank in age and luck. No one

asks friendly questions
or even smiles. We keep politely silent

and hope for news that is not bad.

3) Exposure

Have you ever had radiation exposure?
That question! and again images whirl—

    milk with strontium 90

    x-rays for bronchitis

    working at MIT: yellow barrels
    marked with nuclear symbols,
    rooftop vents I was warned
    to stay clear of—

    every inhale / every taste / every
    open skin pore now suspect

Who on this planet could answer their question
with anything but *Yes* or

Not that I know of.

4) The Appointed Day

Tomorrow I will dial the phone
hear the ring, the greeting,
state my business
be put on hold.

My doctor will be buzzed
decide to use the office phone
settle into the comfortable chair
maybe take a hard candy from the bowl.

He'll reach for the file labeled with my name
spread it open on his desk
pick up the receiver.

All today I rehearse tomorrow, 1 o'clock:
dialing the phone
the ring
stating my business calmly.

Months of waiting narrowed to:

No, he will say
or, *yes.*

The Summer She Decided to Quit

for Sara

Her mother has died.
Who will foot her grief
when she climbs the stepladder
toolbelt across hips?

Pipes to be bent   cut   fastened;
circuits of wire to be pulled—
her lanky torso
                    outstretched to ceiling.

Above the wail of sawblades
and hammers   loud banter about
lottery tickets and last night's
doubleheader. Here: to punch

means   to hug   and an insult
is a warm *good morning*
and everyone wishes she would stop

crying   stop crying
and join in about the lottery
or last night's game.

A toolbox of orphaned emotions scream
home   mama. The cords of her drill
loop down the corridor
                    and out of sight
and everyone wishes she would stop crying.

Chance

for Gloria

For years of faithful apprenticeship
she carries their tools swallows
their contempt and
follows their advice
   roll with the punches
   go along to get along
if you want to make it in this
rough business where the best thing to say
is   nothing. *Shit happens. Don't get mad.*

Not once in three years
asked to join a game of gambling   or chance
not the card pool the check pool check poker
not *Buy some chances on*
a carload of cheer or   50% of the take
not even *You want frozen shrimp*
Three bucks a pound Don't ask questions

until her journeyman pushes her
flesh bouncing off
concrete   down pushes   her   down
the sub-basement stairway   no one around
but them two. That day for the first time
she is offered a chance:
Buy a chance   .357 Magnum for raffle.

She calls God over that night
and the Devil   quizzes them one at a time

then both at once   throwing her questions
like hot coals to catch them off guard.

By starting time tomorrow she needs
a confession. Who designed those choices
    roll with the punches?
    quit her job?
    gamble   .357 Magnum?
and who sent that Raffle Man? Why!

Work Fantasy
(Apologies to the Anti-Nuclear Movement)

Some days *I* would push that button—
Pablo's street shoes flung astride an I-beam,
a klansmen-eating-watermelon cartoon tacked
to the shack door, clit photo, calendar breast,
laughter over wives and girlfriends or just
a word   so common
you   won't   even   shrug. You'll see me
reach into my toolbox, assume
I am switching screwdrivers, grabbing a pliers.

Tell Me

for Karen

What
shall I
do
with the
woman's
hand
left
on the table
of the radial
arm
saw
she was not
instructed
how to use.

It has been
knocking
at the window
of my dreams
poking
in the closet
of my memory
resting
on my shoulder
when I
come home.

What
shall I

do
with that hand
seized
by her
co-workers
and shaken
like an amulet
to exorcise
women
from their midst.

It has been
tearing down
curtains
ringing
bells
writing me
notes
wearing
my rings.

Assembling a Labor Chorus

Quit mistaking me for Mother Mary
coming on bent knee for redemption
I cannot give (as though your

half-hearted confessions, a few jokes
and a Hail Mary and the Union
would redeem history anyway).

And don't dream that I'm Sleeping
Beauty waiting in stillness
for your kiss of attention.

I am Lazarus   wide awake   mouth open
returned with cartons of documents
that list names. And wounds still bleeding
after decades. Time we defrocked
priests   broke the altars   and kissed
the open wounds of the dead. Then
we'll grasp arms and sing *Solidarity
Forever* without a list of exceptions.

Electrical Job at Tent City

The stench
inside our skin
as we un-
screwed
the rectangular
cover   still
left us unprepared
for what we
found: a rat
electrocuted across
live copper.

John grabbed
the head and then
the body half and ran
outdoors   while I   stayed back
in the electric closet
and with a two-by-four

beat and beat
the maggots spilling
pencil-thick and one-inch long
from the metal box.
I thanked
John and

bought his coffee.
I was foreman. The rat
by rights was mine.

UnWelcome Mats
at the Construction Site
for Cher, Donna, and Cassandra

A kick
denting her lunchbox

urine
in her hardhat

dead rat
beside her saw—

indignities that awaken
history's skeletons to come
clattering across the I-beams.

People who look like him
people who look like her

have met before when
the boot the penis the animal

did not stop at petty crime.
He smirks. She raises

a muscled arm, snaps
her fingers and the skeletons

float down beside her like
a band of maracas. Hips swirling around
boxes of bolts   two-by-fours

the coring machine   she merengues
partnered with every horror people
who look like him have committed against
people who look like her

ending beside him. She extends
her arm offers
                a dance
to the rhythms of skeletons
He steps back. Returns to work.

It's a Good Thing I'm Not Macho

(1984)

poems of apprenticeship

Homage

Electricity! at its core
    poetic: the earth herself
an enormous generator.

Electricity! at its core
    political: the human animal
a current-carrying conductor.

Hanging In, Solo
(So What's It Like To Be
the Only Female on the Job?)

On the sunshine rainbow days
womanhood
clothes me in a fuchsia velour jumpsuit
and crowns me with a diamond hardhat.
I flare my peacock feathers
and fly through the day's work.

Trombones sizzle
as my drill glides through cement walls
                 through steel beams.
Bundles of pipe rise through the air
at the tilt
        of my thumb.
Everything I do
              is perfect.

        The female of the species
        advances 10 spaces and
        takes an extra turn.

On the mudcold-gray-no-
sun-in-a-week days womanhood
weighs me down in colorless arctic fatigues
hands me an empty survival kit
and binds my head in an iron hardhat
three sizes too small.

I burrow myself mole-like into my work, but
my tampax leaks
my diamond-tip bit burns out after one hole
my offsets are backwards
all of my measurements are wrong.

At each mistake, a shrill siren
alerts all tradesmen on the job
to come laugh at me.
Everything I do
               must be redone.
    The female of the species
    loses her next turn
    and picks a penalty card.

On most days, those
partly sunny days that bridge
the rainbow sunshine days and the mudcold-
gray days
              womanhood outfits me
in a flannel shirt and jeans
and hands me a hardhat just like
everyone else's. I go about my work
like a giraffe foraging the high branches:
stretching myself comfortably.
As I hang lighting fixtures and make splices
I sing to myself and tell myself stories.
Everything I do
              is competent enough.

    The female of the species
    advances 1 space
    and awaits her next turn.

Through the Ceiling, Maiden Voyage

Sliding
    under an airduct, then
scrabbling crab-like along pipes and crossbars—
    my flashlight breaking
    the darkness, my bodyweight
    placed gingerly (not to fall through)—

I ask the stillness,
has another woman passed
             before me?
to witness this
        pulsation of buildinglife:

arteries of plumbing pipes branch across
electric nervelines   sinews of metal
secure airducts
        pumping coolbreath/warmbreath
to the skeletal framework of iron beams.

How many times I have passed
under ceilings
        unaware
            unsuspecting.

Working Overtime

Midnight.
I am sitting on the cement floor of an elevator mechanical room
on the 17th floor of a deserted officebuilding with four men—
three of whom I met only two weeks ago, the fourth,
just tonight. Drinking Coca-Cola and telling jokes and all
very tired, having worked since seven in the morning.

Suddenly.
I become aware of: sitting here exhausted with four men—
strangers—in the middle of the night—here, where no one could
hear me scream! and I startle myself.

First Day on a New Jobsite

Never again a first day like the
First Day
that Very First one
when only the sternest vigilance
kept the right foot following the left
following the right following the left
each step a decision, a victory of
willpower over fear, future over past.
Margaret's out there   Keep going
She's been working a few
weeks already   She's managing
Keep going The legs buck
LA   Seattle   Detroit   women passing
through construction site gates for the
first time   Keep going Right following
Go home if you want! But
tomorrow   What'll you do for work
tomorrow? left following right up to
the gate
where a man hands me hardhat
and goggles and points me toward a trailer
where the conversation
stops
as I enter:
Well, what'll we talk about now.
Can't talk about girls.

And then Ronnie, the one with beady eyes

and a gimp leg, who knows for a fact—
　　one of the girl apprentices
　　is a stripper in the Zone—
says to my partner *Give me your apprentice*
and I follow him　tripping over cinderblocks
to a small room
　　　　　　　　where he points to the ceiling:
I need some hangers 11 inches off the ceiling
Here's the Hilti
The rod and strut are in the corner
The ceiling's marked where I want
holes drilled and leaves
　　　　　　　　without
　　　　explaining
　　　　　　hanger
　　　　　　rod
　　　　　　strut
or seeing that the bit on the heavy drill
barely reaches
　　　　　　x-marks on the ceiling
when I stand tiptoe on the ladder's
　　　　　　　　　　top step.

Knowing which words to use
what jokes to banter
how to glide the body through dangers
without knocking anything　or anyone;
learning to speak first
and define the territory
　　　　　　　　of conversation.
Passing.

❖

Another
      first day: the job new
the workers all strangers   all men
myself the only 'female'
              and yet
we find, almost easily, the language
that is common:
        —*Get me some 4-inch squares*
           with three-quarter k-o's—
        —*Need any couplings or connectors?*
        —*No, but grab some clips and c-clamps*
           and some half-inch quarter-twenties.

Passwords.
        —*You know what you're doing in a panel?*
        —*Sure.*

Mechanic to mechanic.
Never again a first day like
the First Day.

Wiretalk

Working three floors apart
two mechanics
           at either end of a pipe
feed and pull in meter,
keeping time
through a morse code of yanks and tugs:
fingertips
        against the vocal chords of wire.

Working Outdoors

January:
working early morning hours
against frosted moonlight/
arctic wind
    stabs through clothing/
fingers numb ears
so cold they
        burn/   July:
                 working midday hours
                 under dizzying sunlight/
                 muggy air
                     languishes in the lungs/
                 fingers swell
                 initiative
                     wilts/
winter/the body
            not warm summer/the mind
                          not clear.

Companion

From beneath the angle iron which just
plummeted 24 floors
a chuckling voice: *not yet   not yet.*
Then Death
       disguised as an old Italian laborer
       springs out   skips away

and at that moment's seen balancing at the brink
of the elevator shaft
on 7   where the guardrail's been down
since Tuesday (the carpenters
haven't got back to it). With a wink
and a holler: *not nooooow*

He backsprings

              down the shaft

to the vaultroom where He hides
in high voltage switchgear: *just testing!*

Advice

found poem

A machine is like a woman.
You've got to sweet-talk it
 whisper to it.

If that don't work
kick it.

Warningsigns

Harsh tongues
        soften; gentler tempers
ignite on contact. Rumors
reproduce on the hour—
    Bobby swears seven/Dave heard four/
    Steve is definite: three today
             five next Friday.

          At coffee
John swallows his hot and
    jumps back to work;
Kenny whines about why
    a just-married guy needs a job most;
Curt lectures on 'what he
    never liked about this wormshop.'

Much as a farmer smells an approaching storm
an experienced mechanic can
taste it in the morning coffee break:

layoff today.

Tradition

for Joe and Stanley

Apprentice and journeyman
    in its finely-tuned moments
    a duet:

the nimble range of tireless legs
compliments the pure
rounded tones of virtuoso hands;

the diligent staccato of questions
syncopates the
            meticulously
orchestrated plan.

Harmonies—
    the bass of experience
    the trills of energy—
surpassing the depths
of the solo instruments.

It's a Good Thing I'm Not Macho

If the injury had begun more
high-pitched—
            an opened artery
            a four-story fall—
I would not have hesitated
to see a doctor sooner.

But the action unfolded gently
the pain in my hands
        just a little
                at first
            an easy distraction to ignore;
and the crippling, too, came on
slow-paced—
                no dramatic moment
                spotlighted center-stage—
                so I merely

made adjustments. When the right wrist
no longer moved as I commanded
I transferred screwdriver and pliers
into my left. When the left
began to refuse as well and
not only wrists, but fingers, too
mocked my commands
I used both hands together

and set my alarm clock earlier

to allow extra time
for lacing boots
and opening the lid on the juice jar.

And when mid-act, my hands dropped character
revealing themselves
        swollen and flaccid as warm pudding
        barely recognizable as hands
I pretended not to notice. Critics
will not say this actor faltered.

Maybe if injury were not weakness
and weakness
                lower than woman
I would have seen a doctor sooner.

I waited.

Every few months, still, pain
reminds me with a quick kick:
the show need not always go on.

Limits

She was Most
Likely to Succeed
of the six at start
       the most experienced mechanic
       enthusiastic
       intelligent, but

she came to believe herself paranoid.
She took medication.
At the end of a year
            she dropped away.

Perhaps she was mad as a beached whale.
I do not know.

           I do know
she was not mistaken
when she feared 'brothers'
mocked her and strangers
wished her failure.

We five who
       completed
what she could not

           remembered her
graduation night.

Past the Finish Line

for Sara, Jill, Cathy, and Margaret

Family
neither by blood nor choice
we five
       caught in a welding flash of history
forged a sisterhood.

As students of the mysteries of our trade
we uncovered the phasing of our cycles:
       one falling in defeat signaled
       another
              rising in triumph
and so we carried each other
through sine waves of emotion
re-charging each other's determination
with stored-up capacitance for
                   derision
                   shunning
                   loneliness.

We survived isolation by the law of mutual induction:
       magnetic fields of bodies
       separated physically
       can still overlap and empower.

Where a 100-year curse had vowed
'no woman shall pass here'
we passed:

all five
       as one.

And then
       in the crash of a moment
the five-who-would-not-be-divided
were divided. There are some odds
the most valiant pioneer cannot overcome.
A woman pedaling home her bicycle
is no match
for a drunken man at the wheel of his car.

In the crash of a moment
the five became four
            never again
except in memories and photographs
          to be five;

and yet
      always to remain five.

Margaret   Margaret   Margaret
you call forth our best
a bridge a balance a beacon.

Toward Ambidexterity

Dear Left Arm,

They are true
your accusations.
I did abandon you in infancy
    ignore you
    stifle you
    neglect your training, but
in my defense,
it was the custom.
You were the right arm's helpmate
                    girlchild
                    wife.

Yes, it was the right hand
always the favored one that
    answered mail
    cut the vegetables
    paid the bills
    handled tools

while you—
        coordination unrefined
        strength unencouraged—
grew to diminished adulthood.
Your handwriting, even, is childlike.

Now, those muscles long ignored rise up:
beg to throw a softball, write
a poem, swing a hammer
paint a banner

and you point
                    toward me
                              and accuse—
but how was I to know your
desires you never
spoke up never pushed
your way in or
                    perhaps it was
I did not hear until
                              now
when the tasks are too large
to disregard allies.
Only as a balanced whole
can the body
                    redress history.
You have taught me:
                              all hands are needed.